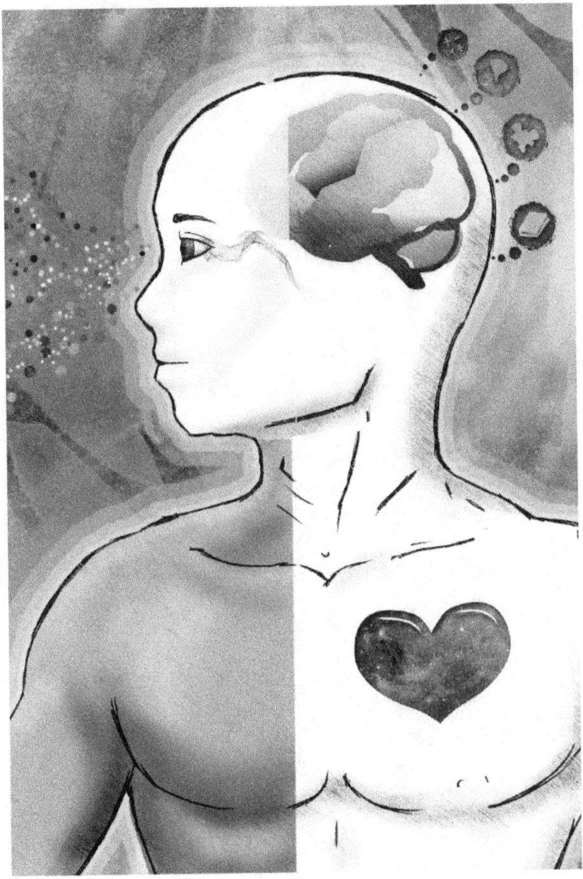

Mind Empowerment

MIND EMPOWERMENT

Mind Empowerment

MIND EMPOWERMENT

Unleash the Power of Your Mind

Instafo

instafo

ISBN 978-1-542-71704-5

Printed in the United States of America

First Edition

CONTENTS

Chapter 5: Stimulating the Mind

Chapter 6: Working the Mind into Shape

Chapter 7: Unleashing the Extraordinary Mind

Mind Empowerment

Mind Empowerment

Chapter 1:

Empowering the Mind

Human Command Center

Our mind reveals a lot about *who we are*, as it leads us in *what we say* and *what we do*. In turn, those around us take note of *how intelligent we are* based on our actions.

However, like most things tend to do, our mind can slowly decline over time, resulting in a loss of some of our mental prowess.

Most people think it is an inevitable part of life when our minds start to fade, but that is not necessarily the case.

What is true is that the loss of some of our intellectual abilities is actually attributed to our lifestyles, as well as our ignorance regarding how to improve them.

There are so many cases of dementia these days, and it is tragic. People who suffer from it feel completely powerless, as the symptom takes over the very core of a person's ability to think clearly, remember things easily, and perform even the simplest daily tasks that once defined them.

The good news is you can find ways to delay such scenarios by learning how to empower your mind and keep it healthy and active for longer! Here are a few of the benefits that you can derive from practicing mind empowerment:

- You'll maintain a sharper mind because you are constantly mentally stimulated, which results in you being more alert and "with it."

- You'll possess information faster (think "supercomputer") because you exercise your brain so much that you can grasp even the most complex concepts with relative ease.

- You'll respond effectively when challenged by a mental task because you don't have to do much digging for answers; they are now coming "off the top" of your mind. (And in those incidents where you don't know the answer? Well, you are happy to learn more!)

Metaphorically speaking, mind empowerment is like giving a boost to a plant that is growing at a normal pace, but you just wished it could grow 10 times faster without bending or drying out. So on top of water, you begin adding in some apple cores and banana skins close to the roots of the plant to make it grow stronger at a faster rate.

Here, the tree is your mind and you are empowering it by adding apple cores and banana skin to its water regimen. Basically, you must add more nutrition to improve the plants' (or your minds') performance and, at the same time, keep it healthy.

Self-Assessment: Mental Engagement Level

Before proceeding on to the different ways to empower your mind, let's do a little self-assessment of how active you are with mental activities.

Pick the answers that describe you best.

1. How often do you read a book or magazine (either in paper or digital format)?

a.) Once a week.

b.) Everyday.

c.) Never.

2. Have you ever come across any of those mind exercises online, and then actually attempted these exercises yourself?

a.) Yes, once or twice.

b.) Yes, it's a regular activity.

c.) No, what for?

3. Have you ever completed a crossword before?

a.) Yes, when computers weren't so widespread.

b.) Yes, I complete at least two of them every week.

c.) No, it's too complicated for me.

4. Do you calculate things in your mind without using an actual calculator?

a.) Yes, but only for the easy stuff.

b.) Yes, it's a great mind exercise (and faster, too).

c.) No, why should I when the machine can do it for me?

If you've picked mostly answer A, then you do engage with your brain ever so often; however, you also do like to take shortcuts, i.e., using technology over brain. This is good to be aware of now because, with time, you will end up relying too much on your clutches and will eventually stale your cognitive abilities. What you need to do is spend more time using your hands, eyes and, most of all, your brain to do basic things like calculating or thinking.

If you've picked mostly answer <u>B</u>, then you are already part of the mentally enlightened bunch. You are constantly seeking knowledge and you love to discuss things like history and philosophy. Your friends consider you the knowledge sponge for you are a natural when it comes to absorbing and articulating thoughts and ideas. You value your brain as your most important asset. Thus, continue on to discover more about how to take your brain to the next level.

If you've picked mostly answer <u>C</u>, then you are a lazy sack of potatoes when it comes to learning and making any mental effort. To you, intellectual discussions are boring (which shouldn't come as much as a surprise since you have nothing to say anyway). You would do anything to get out of hearing your friends talk about the velocity of a moving ball at your next bowling night. You, above all others, could definitely do some daily adjustments to use your brain more and enhance some of your neglected brain functions you may not even be aware of.

Chapter 2:

Never Ending Quest for Knowledge

Added or Faded

Research is prevalently perceived to be reserved for those who are among the intellectual-type. But here's the kicker—don't assume that just because you were "book-smart" back in school means that you are still that way now.

Knowledge must be continually added to and maintained throughout the years.

Research is the most basic and easy way to empower your mind. The problem? Most people today are too lazy to make it a regular, ongoing habit.

One could say that researching helps one to gain knowledge, but it is also crucial to know how to "search" for this knowledge.

Now this doesn't necessarily mean you have to read through piles of scholarly papers. Instead, treat research as a practice to stimulate your mind.

The Research Process

Here's how you can go about your research process:

1. First, choose a simple topic.

2. Then, begin your research by typing the keyword into Google. You will find many results, but focus on

either the top results that pop up in the search engine, or the one that you think is most relevant to your topic.

3. Click on your chosen source and go through it. Next, try to summarize or take notes on the information. The summary should be no more than 50 words. Even with just taking notes or summarizing, your mind is engaged through the explaining of the text in your own words.

4. The next step is to figure out if you have any questions about the subject. Write down three questions maximum. Again, you are stimulating your mind by pushing your investigative abilities.

5. Lastly, open a video journal, where you will voice your perspective like an expert. (If you don't know how to make a video journal, well, guess what? That's another topic you can research on.) This is a great mind exercise to synchronize what you have learned with your own interpretation.

*If you want, you can also join established online forums, or you can organize different discussion groups with friends or colleagues, to talk about the revolving subject(s).

Now it may all sound pretty basic, but the purpose of research is to stimulate your mind by forcing it to actively read, process and interpret information.

Using research as a mind empowerment tool is like training for your favorite sport. You are testing your limits and getting fit both mentally and physically so that you can compete with (and hopefully surpass) others.

In the case of mind empowerment, it is no different than sports in that you want to show the same (or, better yet, superior) skills to combat the opponents. Just, in this case, your opponents are other intellectuals, rather than athletes.

Exercise: Click Search

To empower your mind through research, do it frequently.

You should engage in a research activity at least once a week when you are free (preferably during weekends), even if that means sacrificing some of your time spent in front of the TV, playing video games, or "resting" (being lazy). It can also be a great convenience if you are constantly working on the computer and feel like taking a break.

Here's a subject for you: thermodynamics.

1. Search for this subject online. Focus on the top search results that appear or whichever ones in which you feel would suit what you are looking for.

2. Go through the information and write down notes or summarize it.

3. Make a short video articulating what you have learned.

<u>Chapter 3:</u>

Drawing Power from the Mind

The Real Mind Over Matter

Can you actually enhance your physical performance through mind empowerment?

Visualization being used as a way to strengthen the mind and body was first practiced by Soviet athletes in the 1970s. Before physically performing their respective sports, they would view themselves in action as a way to enhance their actual performances.

Guang Yue, an exercise psychologist from the Cleveland Clinic Foundation in Ohio, confirmed that this technique does yield results after he compared the outcome of physical exercise with the one of mental "physical" exercise. It turned out that those doing physical exercise had 30% muscle increase, while the ones doing mental "physical" exercise had 13.5 % muscle increase.

Quite unbelievable that merely thinking of the actions in your mind can produce physical results as well, right?

Premeditated Process

So, how does it work? First, you use visualization and next, for the sake of results, repetition. With that said, let's put this into action:

Imagine that you had to memorize the following list for the day:

- 6:30: Move the pile of flowers in the backyard.

- 8:00: Call the company to get a quote.
- 9:30: Drive to the train station to get the trip schedule.
- 11:00: Go to the bank and withdraw $1,000.
- 12:00: Dine with my family.

1. First, read the top line and imagine that you are moving the pile of flowers in the backyard. Begin by visualizing the time (6:30), and then visualize yourself slowly moving step by step in the backyard. If you prefer, synchronize each step you take in your vision with your breathing, where one inhale would equal one step, and one exhale would equal another.

2. Visualize the path you follow in the backyard with as much detail as possible.

3. Next, see yourself moving the pile of flowers to a chosen spot (table, barn, etc.). Study how many bunches of flowers you will take at a time.

4. Lastly, repeat this visualization one more time as repetition with the exact steps, details, and procedure in mind. For each step to be precise, you will have to synchronize your breathing and recite as many details as you can.

- <u>Here's a tip</u>: Pick at least five details that you can memorize quickly, and keep those visualizations in your head (for instance, the green portrait in the living room, the blue vase in the kitchen, the old couch in X room, etc.).

Now, move on to the next task (8:00: Call the company to get a quote.) Proceed using the same method: visualizing the time, then the synchronized steps and, lastly, rehearsing the encountered details.

Besides helping you remember what needs to be done the next day, this improves your cognitive ability to memorize things faster. For the busy or "organizationally-challenged" folks, this is a good strategy for you. And for those with memory problems, this is *the* strategy for you.

This can also serve as a way to condition your brain in advance when you have something important to do the next day, week, month, etc. You can use this technique to better prepare yourself, and remember each thing you have to do.

Visualization at Work

Let's use an example. Imagine that a woman has just been hired as a stage assistant during a play. The job requirements are as follows:

- Attend all rehearsals.
- Assist with the collection, organization, and running of rehearsal props and costume pieces.
- Keep the stage clean.
- Set the stage for rehearsals.
- Take line notes.
- Run lines with actors when asked.

- Stand in for missing actors.
- Run errands for the director and stage manager.
- Assist the stage manager in cueing actors, giving calls, setting props, handling emergencies, etc.

Now, for anyone's first day of work, there is always the chance that the person messes everything up because of pressure and lack of experience.

In this example, all of the requirements this woman needs to meet might not take place all at once. Even so, she needs to be ready and empower her mind to get the job done optimally in order for the day to be a success.

1. She needs to visualize the first requirement and see herself attend all rehearsals, keeping note of every detail she sees. She will have to match each breath with every action she takes. She will have to see her gestures and her interactions with actors, including their facial expression, etc. After she is done visualizing the

rehearsal, she will have to repeat the scene one more time (for our repetition phase).

2. She then must visualize herself assisting the staff with the collection, organization, and running of rehearsal props and costume pieces. She will first have to see herself collect props and costumes, visualizing and organizing each one by one, and then allocating them the correct way (to stage right, to stage left, etc.). Then, she will have to repeat this visualization exercise one more time.

She should carry on and proceed the same way for each one of the requirements. She can do this exercise early at home before starting her day (if she already knows what is expected of her), or take a 20-minute work break to visualize it and better memorize what needs to be done throughout the day.

This method not only helps this woman be more productive, but it also helps her memorize what she needs to do even faster. She should remember as many details as she can, which will get her mind stimulated and conditioned by the task beforehand.

Exercise: Mentally Prepared for Mentally Empowered

Now it's your turn to practice!

1. Write down a list of things to do. You can make up one or use a current "to-do" list you keep putting off. An example of a list would be:

- Make a recap of yesterday's activities to give to my boss.
- Assign a list of tasks to the designated staff.
- Call the school director for a school meeting.
(So on and so forth...)

2. Then, visualize each task and assign each one a starting point with either a time or place.

3. Visualization Process - Next, see yourself work through the task by memorizing as many details as you can.

4. Repetition Process - Make sure to stop once you've completed each task, and repeat that task again.

5. Once done, move on to the next task and proceed the same way.

<u>Chapter 4</u>:

Mental Strengthening and Conditioning

Neurobics

There's nothing better for keeping your brain in shape than brain exercises.

Brain exercises, especially those that activate different parts of the brain for increased neural activities, are known to reverse memory loss and improve mental agility.

This is what many professionals recognized, including Dr. Lawrence Katz and Manning Rubin who even came up with the word *neurobics*, which is used to describe mental exercises.

Speaking of mental agility, mental exercises make you use parts of the brain that will help you examine, process, solve and store information. They help you keep your mind alert and maintain your sharp memory.

The right time to enjoy a little mental exercise is while you are drinking coffee in the morning, during your break time at work or school, or before bedtime.

To name a few, the types of mental exercises you could do are chess games, crosswords or word searches, math problems, Sudoku, and much more. Such games are aided in reversing memory loss (commonly seen in those with Alzheimer's) and should be done at least four times a week.

The best way to apply this new weekly routine is to complete the exercises at a strategic time of day when you are not bombarded with "stuff."

Doing these mental exercises has the same effect as doing physical exercises, but instead of you doing aerobics or cardio to tone your body, you are doing crosswords or puzzles to strengthen your brain. Just as you would work out to build muscles and maintain a healthy weight, you can work out your brain to stay sharp.

Let's go through some mental exercises, shall we?

Exercise 1: Numerical Roles

Fill in the empty squares. Sounds easy, but first you must figure out the role of each number. For instance, you may want to know what the number <u>35</u> represents and why it's located at the center.

Give yourself two minutes to figure out what role these numbers play, and three minutes to fill in the empty squares.

9	■	2	■	
■			0	■
	7	35		0
■	28		4	■
7	■	9	■	

SOLUTION:

The number 35 is the largest number and, since it is placed at the center of the cube, each number placed horizontally, vertically or diagonally should equal 35 when they are added up with their counterpart. For example, from the third row at the top you'll add 33 to 2, which makes 35.

9		2		35
	26	33	0	
28	7	35	35	0
	28	26	4	
7		9		31

Exercise 2: Words Formulation

Do this word search puzzle.

E	X	T	L	L	E
I	L	E	N	A	P
Y	A	E	M	O	O
B	X	N	V	Y	O
W	E	A	W	E	L
R	T	G	O	A	N
P	Q	E	S	S	R

1. **First diagonal row**: It's a number made up of the same digit twice.

2. **Third vertical row**: It's the most troublesome years in one's life.

3. **Second horizontal row:** You take one when you are tired in the afternoon.

4. **Sixth vertical row:** It cools you off during the summer.

5. **Fifth horizontal row:** Together as a first-person pronoun.

6. **Sixth horizontal row:** Ready, set...

SOLUTION:

E	X	T	L	L	E
I	L	E	N	A	P
Y	A	E	M	O	O
B	X	N	V	Y	O
W	E	A	W	E	L
R	T	G	O	A	N
P	Q	E	S	S	R

1. **First diagonal row:** Eleven

2. **Third vertical row:** Teenage

3. **Second horizontal row:** Nap

4. **Sixth vertical row:** Pool

5. **Fifth horizontal row:** We

6. **Sixth horizontal row:** Go

Chapter 5:

Stimulating the Mind

Natural Mind Stimulants

One thing that can help give your mind a mental boost from time from time when you're too tired to carry on a task is to give it some mind stimulants.

What do we mean by mind stimulants?

No, we're not talking about those chemical-filled, unhealthy energy drinks and pills widely promoted these days. The ones we're talking about actually come in the form of natural herbs, teas, and infusions, as well as mind concentration tools and even readings.

Ever since a Chinese Emperor and herbalist named Shennong discovered their properties 5000 years ago, teas and infusions have become some of the best natural stimulants for an acute memory. Some of the healthy, well-known stimulants known to provide concentration and help enhance (or empower) the mind are:

- **Ginkgo Biloba**: It's the most well-known supplement to support brain function, thanks to the two compounds found in its leaf: flavonoids and terpenoids. The leaf is able to be purchased in the form of bottled tablets/capsules, or can be steeped in water for tea.

- **Ginseng**: As one of the most popular herbs in traditional Chinese medicine, it not only provides an energy boost, but also supports mental acuity.

- **Gotu Kola**: Although normally used as a tea preparation, it helps promote better clarity, focus, and concentration by boosting blood circulation throughout the brain.

- **Periwinkle**: It should be interesting to know that many of the compounds found in periwinkle can also be found in most medication used for combating dementia like Alzheimer's. An example is Vincamine, which is a medicine used to supply oxygen to the brain.

- **Green tea**: Probably the most popular tea out there, green tea is rich in antioxidants and helps with mental exhaustion and fighting free radicals.

Reading Stimulant

Next on our list of mental stimulants is reading. Professionals like Robert S. Wilson. Ph. D, a professor of neuropsychology at Rush University Medical Center, agree that reading helps stimulate the mind and prevent memory loss issues.

But how does reading do that?

Well, reading engages your mind in the act of comprehending and storing information. Most of all, though, it forces you to piece together concepts, words and imagery used in the author's style of writing to escape reality and immerse yourself in the text (which can, in itself, be considered a mental exercise).

Now, here's how to combine the natural stimulants mentioned before with reading.

First, pick one of the five mind stimulants to consume. Next, pick any text that you will enjoy and start reading. Don't rush and really take your time with this. It is imperative that you find a calm place to read so that you have the maximum mental engagement during this mind-empowering session.

Exercise: Stimulate Comprehension

Let's practice with one exercise and see how it works.

1. Prepare your cup of Gotu Kola (or any of the other natural mind stimulants).

2. Find a tranquil spot where you can sit down and read the following extract from the book, <u>A Journey to the Centre of the Earth</u>, by Jules Verne:

"Perhaps he will tell us that himself."

"Here he is, Monsieur Axel; I will run and hide myself while you argue with him."

And Martha retreated in safety into her own dominions.

I was left alone. But how was it possible for a man of my undecided turn of mind to argue successfully with so irascible a person as the Professor? With this persuasion I was hurrying away to my own little retreat upstairs, when the street door creaked upon its hinges; heavy feet made the whole flight of stairs to shake; and the master of the house, passing rapidly through the dining-room, threw himself in haste into his own sanctum.

But on his rapid way he had found time to fling his hazel stick into a corner, his rough broadbrim upon the table, and these few emphatic words at his nephew:

"Axel, follow me!"

I had scarcely had time to move when the Professor was again shouting after me:

"What! not come yet?"

And I rushed into my redoubtable master's study.

Otto Liedenbrock had no mischief in him, I willingly allow that; but unless he very considerably changes as he grows older, at the end he will be a most original character.

He was professor at the Johannaeum, and was delivering a series of lectures on mineralogy, in the course of every one of which he broke into a passion once or twice at least. Not at all that he was over-anxious about the improvement of his class, or about the degree of attention with which they listened to him, or the success which might eventually crown his labours. Such little matters of detail never troubled him much. His teaching was as the German philosophy calls it, 'subjective'; it was to benefit himself, not others. He was a learned egotist. He was a well of science, and the pulleys worked uneasily when you wanted to draw anything out of it. In a word, he was a learned miser.

Germany has not a few professors of this sort.

To his misfortune, my uncle was not gifted with a sufficiently rapid utterance; not, to be sure, when he was talking at home, but certainly in his public delivery; this is a want much to be deplored in a speaker. The fact is, that during the course of his lectures at the Johannaeum, the Professor often came to a complete standstill; he fought with wilful words that refused to pass his struggling lips, such words as resist and distend the cheeks, and at last break out into the unasked-for shape of a round and most unscientific oath: then his fury would gradually abate.

Now in mineralogy there are many half-Greek and half-Latin terms, very hard to articulate, and which would be most trying to a poet's measures. I don't wish to say a word against so respectable a science, far be that from me. True, in the august presence of rhombohedral crystals, retinasphaltic resins, gehlenites, Fassaites, molybdenites, tungstates of manganese, and titanite of zirconium, why, the most facile of tongues may make a slip now and then.

It therefore happened that this venial fault of my uncle's came to be pretty well understood in time, and an unfair advantage was taken of it; the students laid wait for him in dangerous places, and when he began to stumble, loud was the laughter, which is not in good taste, not even in Germans. And if there was always a full audience to honour the Liedenbrock courses, I should be sorry to conjecture how many came to make merry at my uncle's expense.

Nevertheless my good uncle was a man of deep learning--a fact I am most anxious to assert and reassert. Sometimes he might irretrievably injure a specimen by his too great ardour in handling it; but still he united the genius of a true geologist with the keen eye of the mineralogist. Armed with his hammer, his steel pointer, his magnetic needles, his blowpipe, and his bottle of nitric acid, he was a powerful man of science. He would refer any mineral to its proper place among the six hundred [l] elementary substances now enumerated, by its fracture, its appearance, its hardness, its fusibility, its sonorousness, its smell, and its taste.

*****

3. Read the above extract thoroughly to ensure your comprehension of what the passage is about. You may not know the exact amount of words you are registering as you read, but your eyes are registering them unconsciously. The more you are exposed to new words, the more your mind stores that new information, which expands your knowledge.

4. After you are done, answer the following questions:

- Were you able to fully understand this small extract? Explain.

- What do you like about the story told in this small passage? Explain.

With these questions, we are assessing how well your mind can internally isolate distractions while comprehending written texts.

Chapter 6:

Working the Mind into Shape

Now it's time to go through a series of mental exercises to empower your mind.

Exercise 1: Decipher Words

Solve the following word search:

C	R	O	S	S
X	E	A	A	M
D	L	O	O	T
D	L	S	F	T
P	A	S	T	A
A	C	I	Q	O
P	P	B	C	L

Horizontally:

1. A sacred object.

2. Vikings used to do it constantly.

3. Spaghetti is a type of this.

Diagonally:

1. Snakes are often found inside one.

Vertically:

1. Someone who causes your phone to ring.

2. The present tense of was.

SOLUTION:

C	R	O	S	S
X	E	A	A	M
D	L	O	O	T
D	L	S	F	T
P	A	S	T	A
A	C	I	Q	O
P	P	B	C	L

Horizontally:

1. Cross

2. Loot

3. Pasta

Diagonally:

1. Pit

Vertically:

1. Caller

2. Is

Exercise 2: Interpret Texts

Read from the following PDF up to page 40:
http://publicliterature.org/pdf/bwulf11.pdf

Follow these guidelines:

1. Make some Ginseng tea (or any of the mind-stimulating teas listed in chapter 5).

2. Find a quiet place to read.

3. Read calmly and take your time.

Answer the following questions:

- What is the book about?

- Were you able to see yourself in the story? Explain.

Exercise 3: Identify Objects

We wouldn't talk about mental exercises without bringing some fun into it!

Answer these questions about the painting above:

1. How many people do you see standing?

2. How many people are there total in the painting?

3. How would you describe the background?

4. How would you qualify the main characters in the picture? (Are they rich, city people, poor, etc.?)

SOLUTION:

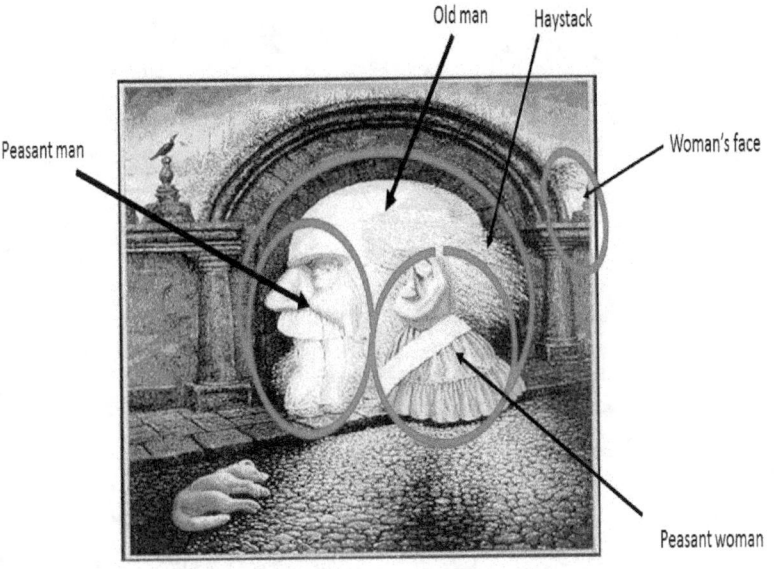

1. There are two people standing in the painting.

2. There are a total of four people in the painting.

3. There are big haystacks in the background behind the man and the woman.

4. The characters seem to be peasants and/or possibly farmers.

Exercise 4: Memorize Performance

Find a schedule or something you feel you will have a hard time memorizing.

Use the guideline highlighting the visualization and repetition process.

For instance, find a starting point with a given task, like the time, and then imagine yourself in action. Match your movement with a moderate heartbeat, and picture moving things and memorizing details so that you can remember them later. Make sure to visualize the scene up until the end. Then, repeat the process one more time.

<u>Chapter 7:</u>

Unleashing the Extraordinary Mind

Less Mental Crutches

Our minds need exercise, just like our body needs it. There is so much to read, and so much to learn. Plus, technology isn't doing us any favors. (Why read when movies are a click away?)

At the same time, we have never been so challenged in terms of our ability to memorize things. Between our endless PIN numbers, codes, hectic schedules, you name it—everything is near impossible to keep up with.

With this fast-paced lifestyle we live now, our minds need to be sharp or we will never be able to survive in this ever-changing environment.

We are a generation who can't seem to keep our hands off our phones, and our access to thousands of technological devices that basically "do all the work for us." However, with all that available, we have become reliant on objects to do the thinking. Therefore, we are not using our brains enough and, as byproducts, have become the ones at risk developing defective brains.

More Mental Activities

Our lack of interest in books and mind-stimulating exercise is causing our brains to deteriorate every day.

Think about how our wise grandparents used to live— playing chess and reading by the fire. Why shouldn't we try to imitate them, from time to time? It worked for them, right?

That's why, from now on, we must take steps to empower our minds.

We can start by memorizing things more effectively by visualizing tasks and repeating them in our minds as much as possible. We should also do research to keep our brains alert and healthy, which is quite a step up from sitting around the house doing nothing. Also, let's do as much reading as we can. And don't forget—natural mind stimulants can come in handy when you need them.

Your journey to empowering your mind has begun! And you can do it!

Mind Empowerment

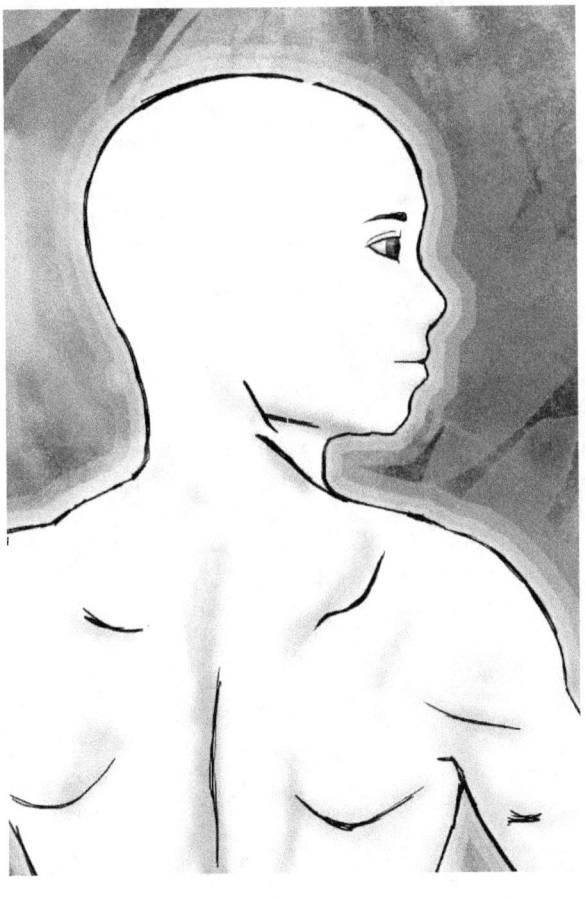

Mind Empowerment